frail the bridge

how frail the bridge
one from another
'tween memory and truth
of what is gone
and what must come
'tween one spark of life
and unknown other

by **Mary Jane Nordgren, D.O.**

dedicated to
kathi, alisa, ted and their precious families
loughlins, pritchards, foxes
and
loved friends of rivers to the sea writers
and writers in the grove

cover design by William A. Helwig

ISBN #978-0-9703896-7-1

CONTENTS

cantilever

modillion

truss

~~~ ~~~ ~~~

acknowledgment of previous publishers of versions:
    alone (as 'mourning,' 4 and 20 Poetry); at the inn at
spanish head (4 and 20 Poetry); goliath of hunger (4 and 20
poetry); hinter (4 and 20 poetry); i hide (Caregiver
Magazine); instinct (Great Poets Across America); old
glory in the wind (Beacon, and Forest Grove News Times);
old tillie (4 and 20); possession (4 and 20 poetry); proem
(Thiel College houyhnhnm); seamed flag symbol (Forest
Grove News Times); sheltered (4 and 20 poetry)

cantilever

instinct

instinct, they say
   touch a newborn's feet to a surface and
      the infant will lift one foot and
        then the other
      as though stepping

touch his palm and
   his tiny fingers will
      grasp and close
  —mere instinct

but when those near-translucent
   hopes for mastery of piano or guitar
      stir and touch, surround my
        pointer to the world's
          past betrayals
          and present heartaches

when fresh, soft delicate skin
   brushes callus and scar
      and clings as though in trust

those vulnerable fingers melt the wrongs
   and promise goodness and mercy
      in a future
        now in my hands

2220 ralph avenue, cleveland 9

the curbs were my limit
>momma watched

curbs of concrete with black tar between the segments
>tar i picked at and chewed
>when momma didn't see

curbs, inches high, that barely contained
>the muddy water when
>the hydrant gushed out a flood
>and momma let us wade

curbs so wide apart that friends could only wave
>until old enough to cross
>and once had rain on the other sidewalk
>while sun baked ours
>even momma had never seen anything like that
>>before

curbs lined ralph avenue where i grew up
>walked to kindergarten
>fell from the oak tree
>learned to skip double-dutch
>balanced my sister's two-wheel bike
>while momma scurried alongside

a home, a neighborhood
>a way of life and values
>as i grew up beside a road
>my momma chose

patterns

momma needed patterns
      needed the world to be ordered the way it was
supposed to be
but i didn't know that for decades—could only see
      that i made her angry with dislike when i was a child

now i hold this skirt pattern in my hand
aware as so many times before in my growing up
      how flimsy is this guide to the way
material should be measured, laid out
      cut to fit

the pattern dictates not from inner strength
but from promise that others have gone before and found
      these measurements, these lines, these directions
      are best at leading one to where one wants to go
tradition has wisdom

momma said so

but i wanted to go somewhere else
my sense of line wanted a different twist
i didn't know i was 'bad'
      or disrespectful for trying
      a slightly different path

you cared for me, i know
the skirts and pj's you cut and sewed

the long yellow dress you made for me
    as princess in the queen's court at berea county fair
            they needed someone small but all front teeth
            at least partially in

that i choose my own way does not mean
that i don't respect your generosity of spirit

my apology now—so many years late—that i did not see
how difficult it was for you
            that i would challenge the foundations
                    of your universe
            that your security depended on 'should'
                    and 'supposed to be'
how callous i was to assume
            you were no more afraid than i was
though i had not lost beloved teenaged sister
            to appendicitis-peritonitis
or clung as bride to new husband driven
            from promised job by the great depression
or held my breath while three brothers were away
            at battlefronts in wwII

forgive me—neither of us was evil
            only ourselves

banister to wisdom

at the head of the flight
of the steep stairs
i climb up and on
my right foot dangling
fifteen feet over narrow
hallway below

i close my eyes
afraid, but determined
i've seen my uncles
and my older sister do this
but i wouldn't try
when they could watch

my palms are slippery
as i try to grip
the dark, polished wood
slowly i ease my near-prehensile
toes from around the decorative
uprights and let
my bum first begin to move

i lift left foot
from its final anchor
and the slide begins in earnest
balled red-plaid dress and
white cotton panties against
the lacquered railing

i clutch at, but cannot grasp

the smooth, wide rail
i swoosh
faster and faster
gritting my baby teeth
to keep from screaming

a gasp escapes my mouth
as i descend, but grandma
doesn't hear me until
i've reached round, decorative end curl
swished near-sideways off it
and clattered to the wooden floor

i'm not crying, exactly
momma would have
rushed to pick me up
and coo sweet assurances
but grandma, mother of
three boys, stands arms akimbo

come over here, and I'll
pick you up, she says
i'd come to you but I have
a bone in my leg
i stagger up, blinking, and
check that i'm okay

next time, don't come down so fast
she says over her shoulder
as she returns to the kitchen
i feel so bad about that bone in her leg
i hold onto the banister as i look back
up its length; so much to learn

no i-phone, pad, pod or 'puter

we played local versions of baseball
      in dusty, tufted vacant field
climbed tall oaks until our weight
      made slender trunk bend like a branch
rode our bikes—unlighted—
      down the alley-hill at dusk
snatched lightning bugs
      from low summer night sky
lowered our eyes and murmured 'yes'm'
      when neighbor lady scolded
cringed but stood when momma spit
      into a hanky to wipe our face from grime
were told 'wait until your father comes home…'
      with trepidation
answered when called, never thinking
      not to
went—with fear but heads up—to wars
      we did not start
met life's maimings without announcement
      to the world
suffered in near silence
      released the fireflies while their light still shone

old glory in the wind

stripes

      of crisp white integrity by
      valorous red ripple
      whipping curves, steep climbs and drops
      like hard roads taken against odd
      winds buffeting, battering, straining
      resources, strength and self-control

stars

      crisp white individuals flutter
      torn from neighbors, alliances
      reclustered, reconfigured
      but unified against blue honor sky-field

challenged, we stand
proudly, we hail
humbly, we serve

seamed flag symbol

i stand beneath, looking up
red, white and blue furling, unfurling, whipping in the
wind
seams stitched by creative hands
joining red to white, white to red
puckers along the stitches
nothing unites seamlessly
individual threads are tortured, disrupted
pulled this way and that
their own bent pressed into service
to the whole
proud, united
as we stand

old testament promise

you will be
as numerous
as the stars in the sky
as grains of sand
          on the beach

this promise to
heroes
not perpetuation of even
these favorites'
lives,
but of his line
her descendants

not 'me'
but 'us'

the 'you' of the promise
is plural

love is

love is an interval within a mystery
roiling under a flared bridge
like opponents in a moment of peace
while all reload

love is aching
to more
than is humanly possible

love is bitterly regretting
weakness, smallness
when growth and strength
would have allowed
airborne wishes
to span the crevasse
to snuggle beside still waters

love is a firefly
flitting in and out of lighted knowing
but mostly flying
in dark morass of
'i'm trying'

dr bill k

on a windy hill
bright california autumn
i met a lion

i want to feel the earth with you

i want to find the path beside the stream
      and climb with you beside the tumbling water
      to go back from now to where it once began
      and see the mountain lake
          you found alone

i want to drink it with you
      and feel as you felt and know
      you give me something of yourself
      i want to feel within me
          what you are

but memories are not as warm as flesh

regrets for pain i caused instead of joy
      intrude upon my dreams
      and dim the warmth of you
      as even the
          grave does not

i want to hold you, love
      i want to embrace the earth with you

alana

nine years, eleven months, four days
each hard-fought
wrestled from the demons inside

no conqueror yet
no straining my arm to
pat myself on the back

but upright, standing stronger
cleaner, almost to zero
nearly acceptable, me

i dared drop in; they'd all invited
alana, sister of our host, was there
class princess, now widow

still looking at me as though I
were hero with the final-second
td instead of dt's—does she know?

the gang, the jocks, fresh-faced no longer
most jowled, thickened; two treating this
reunion as a chance to sell insurance

many toasts to past saturdays; most
assumed i'd kept on winning
alana'd appear from nowhere, tinkling laugh

shifting conversations, avoiding probing
questions; i didn't need to lie
she'd hand me caffeine-free diet coke

settled long enough for the bubbles
to fly away and dark enough to
seem something far more potent

card game time, she blinked
looking at me, but said nothing
she couldn't run interference

was i sure? she squeezed my hand
'lose your shirt at my place,' her eyes said
'not at a friendly hand of poker

'for old times sake, for hard-won
present time's sake, dig your finger-
nails into your palms so pain reminds

of what you value now'
but i'd long bitten nails to the quick
the dead rose lumbering

tales down-wrested truths
strip-pokered me of dignity
i wonder who won my pants?

bill due

cat lies between us
i set her now beside me
i would touch
the man

i want to ask him
but love cannot be demanded
i touch; he draws back
as though from pain

it cost, oh, how it cost
it taught strength
a kind of courage
and blind relief

to feel! so long dead
to watch him breathe
touches me
but it is winter

i hoped, i dreamed—so
now i will not sleep
knowing
he cannot love me

if you really love
set free
i live that, or try
his pain twists my heart

blue eyes, even smiling, lack warmth
what holds him is not
me; in the cold
i watch

he turns, sighs, knowing
it takes time
to let hands unclench
empty

〜〜〉〈

plea

forgive me, darling

oh, love

forgive me

call of a generation

oh, lord, the staggering humor
of pleasure, allured as we are
by bright neon
and undulating skin
like sweet honey-suckle drawing
to itself, sucking
the life of the next generation
from the loins
to be carried
beyond the here
to there
from the now
to the next struggling
life-crazed male
to spread seed
he's assured is his
but birds and bees and flowers know
is the next generation's
imperative
to come into being

we roll and wallow; hump and sigh
moan for the privilege
of staggering under the yoke
of offspring's wants and needs
never seeing the humor
of our bondage
planted and bound in the guise
of pleasure

perfect storm

the world is so big!
i love storms almost
more than sunny days
she laughs
brushing back wet hair

winds fell dead wood
and, moaning,
bend the living

he shivers

fog blinks out the stars
their world
contracts
as though burying
them in ever smaller
coffins

he cringes
cold

whatever warms his soul
she prays
reach and touch him
now
for me

the stars didn't nova
she whispers
they're there behind the shroud

trembling
he shakes off
her hand

≈≈)(

advice

mending nets with gnarled hands
whistling beatles tunes with salt-dry lips
he listens to my lovelorn tale
hummmpffs a bit, fingers slowing
'every couple,' he eventually intones,
'must settle to their own depth
in life's waters'

team a

husband and wife
teamed
against the daily
ruts and crevasses
   of worry, finances, illness
   boredom, weariness
   and fear

determined to plow
   a fertile field
determined to reap
   a loving, supportive home

you have won, ivan and lori
you have won

we have drunk full

we have drunk the wind, my love
        swelled with the rhythm
        of incoming waves
        pounding earthly shores
        connecting anemone, zebra
                —and human

we have felt
        the tumult of birthing waves
        roiled by breezes, currents, tides
        our peace, landed in stars

we've known
        hovering, intense sky
        algid, bleak, raw cold
        embrittled bare twigs scratching
        at ice-laced windows

frost has cemented
        each breath of life
        each inhalation
        burned

you reached out
        reminding me that love
        like life
        is gift watched over
        by angels
                —my love, we have drunk the wind

touch

(a pantoum)

we touch so briefly
gray light fades from
clouds gouged by branches
trembling in deep cold

gray light fades
boughs laden, dragged to breaking
trembling in deep cold
unclench empty hands

boughs laden, dragged to breaking
clouds gouged by branches
unclench hands empty of love
we touch so briefly

i am, and have been

proof of love
and being loved
in the joyous laughter
of my children

retreat

deep joy or pain
  closes our eyes
    against the world

coping one-on-one
  with reality
    requires self alone

i watch my daughter
  close me out
    knowing her pain

knowing how little i
  can really do
    to help her

except to be here
  when again she can deal
    with a world beyond self

(written in the chemotherapy infusions room, Tuality Hospital)

awesome

ceos tout mega-deals
    teens envy brand name sneakers
        children boast of wrist baubles
            plastic, overlaid with
              'gold'

yet, look upon a water drop
    suspended at leaf tip
        pear-shaped by gravity
            prismatic at its fall
                revealing unexpected glory

as we are thinned to infinity
    where we cling
        sever us not
            from one another
              or from You

the gourd, the father and the girl-child

girl-child of rural india
as thin with hunger
as the others of her village
but believing a self
of worth—a fighter
follows her father to market

lone female vendor
she plants callused feet wide
beside her father
holding a single
precious gourd she has
nurtured in tiny rooftop garden

women stare, men scowl
at a girl-child in act of selling
it is man's work
but father has said if profits
are to be her own, then
all efforts must be hers as well

vague threats that she would dare
to take a place not traditionally hers
she inches closer to her father, but
stands her ground beside him
and then a shy smile, a wink
of acknowledgement of courage

more openly a few folks nod
some even look to see her produce
at last, a buyer!
20 rupees in her hand
more precious than glittering gems
this profit of her labor

for father has agreed to let her
press these coins into the palm
of her teacher—to stay in school
perhaps postpone marriage 'til
after puberty, even continue school until
unheard-of legal age of eighteen to wed

ah! such dreams!
father smiles as her fingers caress
the twenty rupees her tiny garden
has raised—a single gourd
thin girl-child of rural india
trembles with joy
          and hope

autistic

'no kisses!'
her granddaughter cringes, and she
shrinks down
rejected

dys

does a mother matter?
 ask the empty children
  of an alcoholic

 judgmental
  because she's never
   known approval

 narcissistic
  because no one
   else exists
    in his unfeeling world

 emotionally volatile
  because she has
   no inner strength
   of surety

 focused into tunnel vision
  because goals
   he can bull toward
    without sneering ridicule

sucking dry

i'm drowning
        in my husband's sea of anguish

i'm withering in resentment
        jealous of his adoration
                of son who works not,
                        neither does he fail to beg, and borrow
i am not free to speak

son latched on, newborn,
        and when she weaned
                by tossing him away
                        in drunken choler
he snared the nurture of
        his father
                demands, receives
                        and punishes for
                                breasts that will not give him suck

when asked, he gives
        and subtly destroys
                something of what
                        he's to care for

i cannot accuse
        the slight damage
                is seen again as accident
                        small price to pay

                    for labor freely giv'n
                        for all that dad has done

it's the accumulative destruction
        of the father

                    ≈≈⊁

i mustn't forget

he loves him—wee son's first toddling steps
      i never saw
tow-headed boy's inquisitive wonder
      i never heard
brash youth's loud triumphs and pale losses
      i never shared

he loves him with memories
      i never knew
and can forgive where i see only
      love's pain and disappointment
i must not forget
      he loves him

pigment

he knows not yet
his pigmentation
dictates that he's unworthy
of love or laughter

his mother folds him
in ample arms
in joy of his being
tickles him with love

she hasn't changed
the world's opinion
for herself, though
she would for him

even if it meant
pain or disfiguration
but what she would
she cannot

she can only surround
his growing in secure
acceptance, seeing who he is
applauding who he will be

how many mothers, aunts
fathers, brothers, uncles
would protect him if
they could

but color brings instant reaction
only love can counteract
until the world sees past
skin-deep to him

〜〜〉〈

the hardest learning

kiss it, mommy
make it better

ah, my love, i'd
give my life to

knowing

"you know," she says
and i do know
but she is young
      to detail the anguish
           of uncaring
           of disconnect
           of losing self
so young to know the terror
      of seeking mirror image
           but seeing not herself

"you know," she sings
of finding self
in music she writes
      profound
      haunting

and once again i marvel
      at the depth in youth
as though that depth
      is plumbed only by
           endless days

laughter of children

squinty eyes
faces crinkled
mouths agape
heads bent back
to roar to heaven

growns edge
closer
to hear
to see
tousled tow-heads
bent together
tears streaming
'cross mud-wiped
cheeks
pudged hands
grip sides
moaning
in ecstasy

adults
close
their eyes
remembering

wizened

wizened by years
    in cold, and dust, and biting wind

       and rising at four to whip
       the chainsaw into roaring
       life as dawn
       brought light to
       work in the woods

wisened by years
    in antipathy, and biting hate

       and raising of three to laugh
       the household into roaring
       life as children
       brought love
       despite the alcoholism
       of their mother

sheltered

(in memory of Charles E. Pritchard, Sr.)

storm roils
candles flicker

"daddy," i whisper

strong arms
     gather me
     in

proem

a blueness, a kind of undercolor he could not name
it was, rather, a presence underneath somehow
that gave the hill a haze of purple blue
as though you could see the water of the earth
pushing to rain upward from the rocks
into the sky

smiling, feeling free in the tautness of toned muscles
his body warm and part of the gold and brown of the grasses
and the green of the hills tinted with the blue beneath
but not entirely submerged
warm and alive

he felt for words as though having no way to describe
what he saw, this was trapped within him—and more
for what he could not name, even to himself,
the shades, textures: depth of the hill—as though
even the color itself had depth apart from the hill—
roughness that would be soft to the touch if only
his fingers could move down over the surface of the slope
could tender the hill as of weave of homespun

knowing he could never caress the mountain
as a whole but imagining from the aspects of its parts
leaving an aching, unable to say what he felt
and thus barred himself from further feeling, and seeing

subtle redness, too, coursing through, not spread out
as was the blue, not diffuse, but somehow vesseled

he smiled, considering
like blood, like blood pulsing through the hill
and the hill alive

alive? beating? was there motion he could not see?
was there breathing, a gentle rise and fall
he could not comprehend?

he held himself still but could not perceive
was it alive with time he could never possess?
time long beyond his span
each beat, years
gentle rise and fall of breath, movement
of a thousand ages —
        an evening gone

now the blueness seemed gathered in veins, as well
large, distended veins, gorged with blood in the fullness
of a breast painful with milk
he sighed, remembering

hers had been
he had traced the blue with his fingertips
felt the softness and the hardness
milk quivering to stream forth
textured veins, separate from the skin, yet part

fine gold and brown hair that fell
over him as he lay
beside her, their babe between them

he'd felt, and watched, and longed
to name, to keep

she called him
and he heard the wind
but could not name
could only be
knowing he was mortal

interface

ah, such an entity as truth
resplendent, unobtainable
by mere mortals of which
i confess, i am one
i came an original of sin
or spitted image of
the sire of creation
i grub the earth, smear
dirt on one and all
in rancor or in joy
'tween heav'n and hades
'tween void and infinity
warmth and cold
insight and ignorance
loyal friend and betrayer
source of pride and dismay
my soul, author of all i
understand, and figment
of a higher being's
twisted imagination
on solid ground, mere
empty space between
distant atoms
i lie

modillion

myopia

in the state of myopia

live a little old lady

and a little old man

and a little young lady

and a little young man

and a little big boy

and a little big girl

and they constitute the majority

〜〜〜〜
〜〜〜〜

suitable

if clothes make the man

would a rag whisperer

pick and choose

to sew up my dream?

madonna metallic

(a pantoum)

madonna, mother
once sweet nurturer
of compassion and care
now material girl

once sweet nurturer
now galvanized breasted
material girl
suckling universal solvent—greed

galvanized breasts for
self-consuming spawn bereft of belief
suckling universal solvent—greed
see only *now* and thus dissolve

self-consuming spawn bereft of belief
in compassion and care
see only now and thus dissolve
suckling our new madonna, mother

trails of self

(a pantoum)

muddy paw prints
trail across the trunk and roof
of the midnight blue corvette
insult, if not injury

stalking across the trunk and roof
the cat disdains status symbol
spooring insult, if not injury
on our showy insecurities

disdaining the coveted status symbol
of the midnight blue corvette
untouched by insecurities
cat trails muddy paw prints

carpenter's tool

flattened to prevent escape
and thus with elongated lead
to give long service
and seldom require sharpening
for his ambition to erect
his place in competitive world

her curves graded, razed
is 'carpenter's wife'
her only epithet
her obit
as she is laid, finally
to rest
in efficient narrow
coffin that costs
gravediggers, too
less bother

squint brick

rough hewn
>straw and clay

variegated surface
>red-baked, or yellow
>orange, magenta

gutted, holed, asterisked
>smoothed, scored
>laced for decoration

prettified
shaped to fancy—for fancy
or to fill a need
scrupulously designed and shaped
to be as needed, wanted
>wished
>desired

allowing air flow
catching the eye
>proclaiming wealth
>luxury, importance

drawing envy

squint
>to narrow focus

this, precisely this
>no other

look at me
squint
>never mind the whole

see me, shaped
      to what i want
      to show
      off
squint
      be blind to mouse
      droppings on the sumptuous
      hallway of this, my
      brick home

chimney sweepings

random wailings of wind
divided by flue partitions
aching moans deduced
from patterned extensions
of lives buried
within bricks of corporate
uncaring greed blessed
by a cardinal number
of self-righteous elite

corporate raiders

they thundered
    and our watchdogs whimpered
        and threw open the gates

they roared
    and our pensions were served up
        on silver platters with golden parachutes

they gnashed their teeth
    and productive businesses were dismantled
        gouged, slashed, clawed and sold
            for profit—theirs

    goods and processes were shipped
        in exchange for commissions, fees
            and paper wealth—theirs

they salivated
    and rape spawned children of greed
        who also chuckle over the bones
            of workers' dreams, and lives

we were wrong about paper tigers

goliath of hunger

hunger thirst tears
hunger listlessness whimpers
hunger gnawing ache

     my breasts dangle, useless to
     my babe with swollen belly
     too dry now for tears
     too quiet to raise your eyes to follow movement
     too resigned to respond to my smile
         if smile i could

i birthed you
i did not want you to die in my arms
but i cannot fight the goliath of hunger

〉〜〈

drawing water

*(to Dr. Barbara Gibby on her work
digging wells for Ugandan orphans)*

the pictures of children
candid shots of grime
      grins
      huge, dark, matted eyes
      stick arms and legs
      protruding bellies
nearly half are girls!
      in shapeless blue/white checked
      uniform dresses
boys in baggy shorts
      over knobbed knees and
      gnarled bare feet
children, not posing, not primping
      just smiling, snot-nosed

shouts of welcome
      'to our viz-a-tores!'

children running to show
      the swamp water
      a mile from the school
where they wade in
      on latrine-soiled feet
      to fill their yellow jerry-cans
      and carry them back
      tall on their heads

to share their meal of porridge
    and speak—shyly—in odd english
    of their schooling
    and their hopes

one—too tired now to speak—
    holds a hand-printed sign of welcome

    by morning, she is dead

charlie's smiling angels

(Charles Taylor was among the first to kidnap and use child soldiers
in Liberian tribal wars. Boys who were even suspected of backtalk
might have their lips sliced off as punishment)

'he killed my ma
he killed my pa
but I will vote for him'

and charlie taylored
landslide victory
three quarters of the vote

spoiled, perhaps
by the maimed who, without hands
could no longer mark their 'X'

or applaud the warlord
president they had followed
from abduction to adoption

bearing arms and
killing love
in order to survive

grinning now in perpetuity
lips severed
teeth bared

struggling to understand

(after the Boston Marathon bombings
April 2013)

is there no 'why'?
or is it that we cannot fathom
beyond our own assumption
of universal truth
that life
if not sacred
at least is valued?

is it not nature
rather than merely nurture
that we cherish
the sanctity of being?

could it be true
that someone for whom
life is cheap
could place his debris-laden bomb
near a child
not much older
than his daughter

and blow off her legs?

quarry

still, yet ever
suspended in liquid space
swimming 'til cramped
gathering self to knead
knotted calves
extend, then flex, clawed toes
chill water
deep quarry
hewn rock walls harboring
resentment to be bared
blocking out
all lingering sunset
looming, gathering dark
to promise colder-yet reception
for my contorted frame

yet still
with threat of quicker pain
they clamber above leering
        granite faces
rifles in hand
flashlights feeble
        in such darkness
but fatal if their sweep discovers

my water-treading nakedness

i suck in breath as
pale gloom-piercing beam

stabs close

then explode in silent scream
as snake slithers near
atop the water

ᚻᚳᚻ

resenting

wrapped in empty

shrink-wrapped in dissatisfied

smoldering, she cringes

to hear her oblivious tormenter's

blithe laughter

possession

it isn't what i have
but what i am that matters
i do little shopping

truss

alone

we feel so alone

but generations

have crouched beneath the sound
of wind
moan-seeking among
writhing branches

have started as shrill
fledged murres
shriek 'me!'
above the roar of incessant
wave upon wave

have heard sobs
in the rain
before knowing
they
are weeping

smile universal

eye contact—you and me
a person somewhat ragged
but a child of God, you see
you hand me a tray of food

at your warm smile and bright eyes
i startle, but only
for a moment
there's warmth between us

my fleeting gasp of surprise
is only because it's seldom
that someone sees me
without looking quickly away

a tray of food you hand me
the food is needed, vital
but that smile of acceptance
gives more than physical health

you've acknowledged the me
i'd near given up on
is there hope that He
can find and forgive me, too?

miniaturized loss

does the ant rue
in the moment of
impending giant footfall
sole-shaped black sky
lowering
regret prom unattended
marriage vows unsaid
children unbounced on
      slender knee

does his life flash
before his eyes
as darkness envelops
his world-space
crushing
regret avowals unwhispered
sugar crystals untasted
hills unbuilt, his mighty power
      now squashed

ah, how much of life
is ours alone, how much shared
in lives in larger or
smaller spaces
differing
time scales, unstudied
unappreciated simply because
not ours, therefore could
      never be

there's a tree on the downhill slope

edging away, the meadow slopes down
    to a bent, wind-maimed tree

sometimes, as a child deliberately, deliciously
    courting mayhem and destruction
    —but not too close—
        i rolled

i was eight before i let go of peeking and stopping myself
    before i banged into that tree

i'd hit it before, of course
    —even a few times with tight-shut eyes—
    but always i'd checked my tumbling descent
        never trusting that the tree would stay
        in my path

i'd never rolled unheeding toward those entangled,
massive roots
    'til glenn dared me, called me chicken
he only learned years later what his slighting remark
    had made me do
        to test my mettle

fool kid! he'd yelped, peering past that stunted tree
    over the cliff to boulders strewn
        at the beaten edge of the sea
        a hundred feet below

i'd done it
      laid myself carefully at the top
      wiped my dripping nose
      closed my eyes
            willing the hero in me not to peek
      pushed off with dry palms and shaking heel
      trusting—in what? in whom?

but glenn is dead to a roadside bomb
      and i feel i need
            to do it now again

)(♎)(

the poles have shifted

how to tell you the upside-down
inside-out, north-is-antarctic
i'm not who or what
i always thought i was

please don't judge me now with
reason, as you see reasonable
my foundation is quicksand
my values irrelevant

my love's a snare to trap me
into yet another round of
humiliated pain that's brought my kids
within range of his fist

please don't yell, or moan, or advise
i know what you say is true
i tell it to myself every other minute
but for now there's only loss

of dreams, of hopes of even the illusion
of being able to protect my children
i'm upright, but i cannot take a stand
please, just listen—and love

old tillie

like the nineteenth century lighthouse

atop rock scarp off oregon's shore

she is battered by his sneak waves

     of betrayal

ℋ♎ℋ

cold hearted

hate chills the marrow

freezes fountains of joy

and contracts our landscape

we huddle to escape

this old body

used to peel navel oranges
     before the rotting thumbs

used to leap from bed or chair
     before the aching spine

used to brush luxuriant dark hair
     before silver overcrept

used to lope miles or dash up stairs
     before the breath came hard

used to bump and bruise and laugh
     before hurting reaching the brim

but has served me well these decades
     giv'n me window to frame

to dare experience, adventure
     to love, laugh—and cry

to hold, and to release
     watch grandkids grow

     thank you

superstition

mother is leaf and mold
       ashes and
       universal dust

why then do i watch
       my steps
       avoiding crack

to save a spine which
       no longer flexes
       or extends

loving, welcome reaching
       flour-dusted hands
       giving cake

and bread of life
       staff of comfort
       gone, now, beyond

i hide

i hide
    at first in guilt
    taking something for myself
    when his needs were
        so much greater

i tremble
    watching him stumble
    seeing his frustration
    hearing his fear
        at each new loss of self

i ache
    wanting to help
    wanting to be more
    for him
        for me

i pray
    for him to accept
    the humiliation
    the dying of each part
        of himself

i weep
    guilty of frustration
    of lashing out, drained
    unable to heal him
        or me

i hide

      to sleep through the night
      to peer at the ocean
      to listen to the wind's song
          to re-know joy

)(♎)(

stepson vs. the wall

someone there is who does not love a wall
    who sees not the protection
        the shelter
            buttresses, sustains, encourages

someone there is who knows only dad
    is no longer an easy target
        for all he has had only to mention
            to be assured of getting

someone comes good-naturedly when asked
    he helps—but accidentally leaves behind a mess
        nearly in excess of his aid
            to be cleaned, repaired, replaced

he leaves—whether his father is well or ill—
    he's done whatever was asked of him
        and will not see the danger or the pain
            he leaves his parent in

someone there is who blames the wall
    who chinks at it, kicking, sniping
        quietly so daddy will not hear
            a bit afraid of daddy taking sides

someone there is whose love-hate rose
    long before the supportive wall was built
        teetering, but still standing
            beside a precipice of ill health and age

they see the shell

they see the shell
the remains of ninety-five years
of high-climbing and logging
of logging, laughing
loving, lifting
lofting golf balls
      often thirty-six holes a day
      in his last two decades
losses he hid

his middle-aged children
see daddy, who
always gave and gave
and now will surely
rise again to give
daddy

i see past the cadaver face
and wasting muscles
to the man who's shared
disappointments, loss —
      and joy

i see his pain
as they cannot
      will not

ransom

ransom my being
      by helping me forget

forgiving their endangering
      him is beyond me

♓︎♎︎♓︎

seeds of...

what verdant or blighted tomorrow
springs not from the seeds of
yesterday's truth—
      or lies?

scarp

my mountain of a man
crumbling now
slipping along faults
engendered over nine decades
granite will sliding
into bewilderment
still remembering my face
but forgetting the day
the questions asked
        and answered
moments ago
lifting rheumy eyes
in frustrated anger
with himself because he
        is no longer who
        and what
                he was

where months and years
of strength
have tumbled into
        the sea of time
and he is left
bald, raw, naked
        vulnerable
comforted only
        by accepting love

my love's slow dying

warmth-seeking
>with chill of nearly
>>a century in his bones

riddled with aching
>teeth clenched against pain
>>of leg spiral-fractured

every movement
>however necessary
>>brings swallowed scream

wanting only comfort now
>and words of grateful assurance
>>and love

pale fire

pale fire
>> where once the flame
>> burned tall and strong

consuming
>> cowering darkness
>> and penetrating chill

not yet embers
>> his flame has moments
>> of flaring life

ashes now
>> consummation as sparks
>> fly upward

cinereous tongues
>> of flame sear memories
>> into my soul

branding me
>> with loss-to-be and chill
>> bereft of his warmth

bereaved

i turn on my side

look across our bed

where he

no longer lies

full moon

mourns

distantly

⠴⠵⠴

at the inn at spanish head

swirling gray
white throbbing
against grained shore

last time we dined out
       was here

he's gone now
       into time

i sit
       observing eternity

numb in my grief

numb in my grief i stumble along
        bewintered oregon shore
  gusts of errant wind scour rocky coast
        with sodden sand and spray
            and then grow quiet

sun shafts filter from glaucous clouds
a gentler wave encroaches upon the wet-packed sand
        the edge of the ocean laps at my toes
            tosses foam ahead in swirls
                gold- and silver-streaked
                    like honey-brown hair
                    upon a darkened pillow

lyn! i cry

be still, i hear

closing my eyes, i struggle to breathe
        i open them, peering at rocks
            and wind-bent hags of trees

the battered sand
        the foam dispersed
            wave retreating
                into ever-pulsing sea

the sun is hidden beyond
        roiling thunderheads but
            its glory

glistens cloud's silver rim

be still, i hear
    be still
       and know that
         I am God

)(♎)(

pier

(a pantoum)

'tween furrowed earth and fluid perpetuity
within the onslaught
of tidal flux
now drowned, now bared to sun

within the onslaught
condemned to rot and death
now drowned, now bared to sun
mussel-bound and barnacled

condemned to rot and death
intersecting stubborn life and loss
mussel-bound and barnacled
jutting into infinity

intersecting stubborn life and loss
of tidal flux
jutting into infinity
'tween furrowed earth and fluid perpetuity

bridge of leaves

a grunt; a word
meaning shared
idea expressed, risked, enlarged
communication
       a joining, dispelling isolation
belonging, support
ideas deepen, concepts grow
lore

generations unhearing
again alone

petroglyph, symbol
written word
a page
       a book to span human lives

bridges of leaves

hate and water find

seek
seep, sweep
nuzzle, pummel
spread
bother banks
nibble at roots
gnaw at foundations
  hard-won over years
  of learning, finally,
   to trust

slinging mud
engulfing the low-lying
stripping bare branches
  naked white like
  bones of the long dead
widening through every breach
  each vulnerability
hiding true landmarks
lapping at character
leaving no former gate
  or bridge
no path
  to reach you
leaving only
  higher ground

haunting beauty

reaching for something within
that knows we cannot touch
let alone control

it leaves us vulnerable
subject to we know not what
fear to submit to

yet long to at least glimpse
a waif of color and near shape
aching to our sight and heart

would give treasure to
loll on tongue, capture a taste
we'd only dreamed

hear in chords what we
catch as fleeting strain, remember
as at birth song

breathe in, engulf our soul
in what we fear will drown us
yet yearn to join

"beautify is truth, and truth, beauty"
if only we could trust
that beauty is good

hinter

what you don't admit
slithers behind you
growing

ﾒ♎︎ﾒ

insight

through pain we
gain wisdom, or
is it through wisdom
we find pain

as he lay

he said he loved me as he awoke
aching, i sat near, holding his hand
had watched as, little by little, abilities carried away
flesh-eating age winning over the years
he was surrendering finally, after courageous fight
he lifted his head, eyes pale blue
he'd awakened from dying to laugh with me
he'd awakened from dying to laugh with me
he lifted his head, eyes pale blue
he was surrendering finally, after courageous fight
flesh-eating age winning over the years
had watched as, little by little, abilities carried away
aching, i sat near, holding his hand
he said he loved me as he awoke

moment in time

a moment   a scream   disjointed time, without root or
perspective
     and then pain
     anguish
     regret
     whispers from deep within, 'if only...'
but there is no way home
     only living
     and dying
     each succeeding hour with that moment
     bloated in your gut

'i want it back!'
'not fair!'
'i want a do-over!'
     probably not
     does it matter to the universe?
     does it matter to your god?
     did you even know your god before that moment?

and there it is: the challenge
     to seek
     to find
     to know
     'knock and it shall be opened to you...
     seek and you shall find...'

a promise

the promise, if you have courage

enough already

gimme an e

    elective. like a choice in college courses. choir vs.
    visual arts/ photography
    only here it's between going under a knife
    sucking up poison
    or doing nothing and allowing
    my body to be eaten away from inside
        wonderful options

gimme an n

    nerve. visualize those nasty misanthropic cells
    give them faces and personalities: meanies, bullies
    —the nerve of them to attack
    my unsuspecting, innocent healthy cells!
    do i have the nerve to fight back?
    and fight back? and fight back?
    the nerve of you even to ask. of course i do!
        i have to

gimme an o

    open. everything is out in the open
    even what i wish—i long—to hide
    like the gap in my coverage. insurance. hospital gown
    if there ever was privacy,
        there isn't any more
    i am visible, vulnerable, poked, probed, x-rayed,
    imaged, scoped, laid bare
    i am an open book with or without benefit of cover
    i'm laid open—
        warts, farts and all

gimme a u

you who hide from me, i'm still me
i'm not contagious. or guilty
i'm not being punished
and you won't be either, for
associating with me
but neither am i deaf to your whispers or proof
against your pity
i'm just me
hurting and scared
and irritable
and in need of your understanding and forgiveness
that i cannot always measure up at any given moment
i may be busy fighting this
and not be paying enough attention to you. i'm sorry
it can't be helped
but i still care
please try me again later?

gimme a g

goodness
so many good people in my world
people who don't know me, but who reach out to help
people who accept my grouchiness, who care
even when i can't thank them because i am
ground to a halt
unable to take care of my own basic needs
people who treat me with dignity despite
my humiliation and their discomfort
gracious.
so many. thank you

gimme an h
  help. i can't help myself let alone…
  e- n- o- u- g- h! whaddya got? enough!
  enough already.

  i have enough
  enough choices if i have the nerve and the courage
      to choose
  i'm open and vulnerable to you, but you are to me, too
  goodness knows i can try to choose to see
      and appreciate
  i can summon up the nerve to face my reality
      and the persons around me
  focus on what matters

      and let the rest go

a writer matters

(after reading Pat Schneider's HOW THE LIGHT GETS IN)

truth of how it really is
changes the world
alters perceptions
widens perspectives
huckleberry's fiction-truth
was a crack in façade
of 'should be, therefore is—must be'
gently tugged self-secured blinders
from not only tom
but also corseted role-players, now unsafe
because the possibility exists
—even if only in tale—
that all's perhaps not right with the world
kids steal, not because they are heathens,
      but hungry
families send forth their sons to slay or die
      to avenge a slight to grandfather
      not even he remembers
"couldn't be!"
they shake coiffed heads
in befuddled disbelief
but huck's adventures make them
peer around the edge of blinders
see now what they have observed
hear now a faint echo
of what they've stopped their ears to
pot-bellied toddlers are not stuffed full
      but starving

whimpers may not be mere whining
        but grief for health and life
cruelty exists against the weak
not just in business
but in poverty-despoiled life
could it be true?

could beloved
becky's cherished innocence
endangered
be but small tragedy
against bayoneted infant
or whole families weighing less
than my muscular son?
cracks in my hard-bound fantasy world
erected out of, not so much greed,
as out of fear there won't be enough
for me
to have what i want when
i want it
impenetrable construction, proof-tight
until
a tinge, a reflection of possibility
enlightens, if only as fiction
twain was yegg of the monolith
of 'cannot be so'

music of the spheres

less than fine mist
     still it fills our souls
it nourishes, though insubstantial
it fills our being, though merely
     puffs and blows of air
     vibration directed
to waiting hammer, anvil, stirrup
     and mind set for pattern
notes of no substance
     echo within us
     lifting to hope, to promise
music, like life, convinces
     of a whole in which
we have worth
     if only as a figment

wellspring

wellspring of joy
      —mine since first i knew i was a person—
            bubbles up
its tinkling, burbling
      sound soothes deep within me
            and i know what matters
i know i matter
      i am part of something so much greater
            quiet, powerful, just being
but my wellspring isn't magic
      doesn't force itself upon me
            or even call me back when i wander off
not indifferent, it cares
      but will not use its force
            it simply is

i go about my busy-ness
      commitments, demands
            i won't remember next week
i fuss, i hurt, i am embarrassed
      by what i do and angered by
            what is done to me
i storm, i mutter
      deafened
            by my surroundings

and then a glimpse of great blue heron
      or wisp of streaky cloud, plaintive coyote howl
            my grandson's giggle—and i remember

i need to move back
      let go of here-and-now to go sit
         beside my wellspring
i need to know that i belong
     and am secure in
       so-much-greater-than-i

)(♎)(

drink the wind, love

   swell with

     incoming waves

  living is so full!

Made in the USA
San Bernardino, CA
21 November 2014